Portishead

in old picture postcards

by
Kenneth Crowhurst

Second edition

European Library - Zaltbommel/Netherlands MCMLXXXVIII

Acknowledgements:
My thanks to friends in the Local History Group of the Gordano Society and to Mr. Jim Ashford for their valuable assistance in the production of this book; also to Mrs. P.M. Bishop for the loan of photographs included in it.

About the author:
Kenneth Crowhurst was born at Tilbury, Essex, and was educated at Palmer's School at Grays, Essex. He first lived in the West Country when he was evacuated to Wiltshire in 1940, but did not permanently settle in the West until he moved to Portishead in 1970 through his employment as an accountant in the Civil Service. His interest in photography led him to collecting local postcards, and he is a member of the Local History Group of the Gordano Society.

GB   ISBN 90 288 4562 3 / CIP

© 1987 European Library - Zaltbommel/Netherlands

European Library in Zaltbommel/Netherlands publishes among other things the following series:

IN OLD PICTURE POSTCARDS *is a series of books which sets out to show what a particular place looked like and what life was like in Victorian and Edwardian times. A book about virtually every town in the United Kingdom is to be published in this series. By the end of this year about 300 different volumes will have appeared. 1,500 books have already been published devoted to the Netherlands with the title* **In oude ansichten***. In Germany, Austria and Switzerland 650, 100 and 25 books have been published as* **In alten Ansichten;** *in France by the name* **En cartes postales anciennes** *and in Belgium as* **In oude prentkaarten** *and/or* **En cartes postales anciennes** *150 respectively 400 volumes have been published.*

For further particulars about published or forthcoming books, apply to your bookseller or direct to the publisher.

INTRODUCTION

Portishead occupies a splendid position on the east coast of the Bristol Channel, some eight miles west of the City of Bristol and two miles from the mouth of the River Avon, commanding a superb view up and down the Channel and across to the Welsh hills and mountains. It lies at the northern end of a ridge of downland which stretches along the coast to Clevedon four miles away, rising to over 350 feet, and its present day houses spill down both sides of the ridge to the Channel shore on the western side and into the Gordano valley which lies to the east. Until Portishead docks were built in the 1870s, the village was served by a sheltered tidal creek or 'pill' which was doubtless one of the attractions to the first settlers who arrived during the Iron Age, some 2,000 years ago. This 'pill' was subject to extreme rises and falls in the water level however, because the Bristol Channel has the second greatest fluctuations in the world – spring tides create a range in excess of forty-two feet at Avonmouth.

In her 'Portishead Parish History', Eve Wigan suggested that the name Portishead could have been derived from the Latin 'portus' (harbour or port) combined with the Anglo-Saxon 'hafod' (head). The present day spelling dates only from the mid-seventeenth century however – at the time of the Domesday Book it was spelt Porteshev and during the following centuries was written in various ways such as Portesheved, Pratteshyde, Porteshede or Portshedd before acquiring today's spelling.

Some traces of earlier visitations in the form of polished stone axes dating from the Neolithic period came to light during the excavation of the Marine Lake, but the first firm evidence of permanent residence in the area appears to be the Iron Age camp on Woodhill. Settlement also continued during the period of the Roman occupation – evidence of this was discovered in the grounds of Gordano School in 1956 when excavations revealed a group of three buildings constructed in local stone with a water supply and a cistern; traces of iron and lead working were also found there.

Men and women doubtless continued to fish and farm the area during the following millenium, but there is no written record of their existence until the Domesday survey was carried out in 1086. The survey showed that Portishead, part of the Portbury Hundred, was a relatively poor community of thirteen peasant farmer-fishermen with a mill, probably powered by the Welhay stream running down the Combe to join forces with the slow-moving Yeo which drained the Gordano valley.

It may well have been the Saxons who built the first sea wall in an attempt to prevent the high tides from inundating the valley twice a day and to reclaim the land, but it was not until the early nineteenth century that the outer, longer sea wall was built and that the marshes properly drained. Only then could the villagers sleep safely on stormy nights – many generations had suffered from flooding in their simple dwellings along Mill Streete, later to become High Street.

Life in Portishead probably continued in much the same pattern during the succeeding centuries, but with a gradual growth into sea trading (Customs officials were first appointed in 1364), boat-building and repairs, because the sea was the only practicable means of communication for the community tucked away in the north-west corner of Somerset, located off the beaten track. The only kind of event likely to cause any great excitement would be a shipwreck, when all able-bodied villagers would rush off to the shore of the Channel to see what spoil could be found. Eve Wigan's book vividly describes a possible sequel to the wrecking of 'La Mariote' on the Monmouth coast in 1331 when a Bristol merchant lodged a complaint against the parson of Portishead and other respectable villagers for carrying off his cargo of Bordeaux wine and other merchandise washed ashore on the local beach. It was not until the early seventeenth century that events took place which were to have a great influence on the future development of Portishead.

The City of Bristol had by then become extremely wealthy from the profits of trade and shipping, and regarded the ownership of land to be the safest investment available. The Corporation accordingly began to purchase land at Portishead and in 1616 acquired the Manor of Portishead with its manor house, now known as Court House Farm; three years later it bought the manor of North Weston with its manor house, The Grange. A century later, most of Portishead, Woodhill and the Down had been added to the Corporation's estates.

In the early nineteenth century, the City decided to develop Portishead as a seaside resort, as a residential village for Bristol businessmen looking for places to live outside the city, and as an industrial centre. The Royal Hotel, opened in 1831, was one of the first examples of municipal enterprise in an age when private development was the norm. During the Victorian period, steam packets, railways and roads all brought visitors to Portishead to stay in lodging houses and to enjoy the simple delights of the seaside – simple because there were no attractions such as promenades or sandy beaches, and very little safe bathing. Most visitors came just for the day, perhaps combining a train or steamer trip with a picnic.

Around the turn of the century until about 1918, a craze developed for sending picture postcards, not just pretty views, but photographs depicting all aspects of life in town and country. Visitors to Portishead were no exception to the craze, as this book proves.

This selection of old postcards, published by both large commercial suppliers and Portishead's local photographer Mr. E.H. Wright, takes the reader on a tour of the village commencing at the church, along the High Street, around Woodhill and along the coast to Redcliffe Bay before returning inland. The book gives a glimpse of the more leisurely way of life enjoyed in Victorian and Edwardian times in what is still affectionately known locally as 'the village' or Posset.

Bibliography:

Anon. *Portishead Methodist Church 1887-1937, A Jubilee Souvenir;*

Anon. *A short history of Union Congregational Church, Portishead, 1877-1957;*

Bond & Fardon, *The Portishead Guide and Visitor's Handbook,* published by the authors, Portishead, 1855;

Bristol Mercury, *Bristol Mercury Series of cheap Guide Books – Portishead,* William Lewis & Sons, Mercury Office, 1884;

B. Brown & J. Loosley, *The Book of Portishead,* Barracuda Books Ltd., Buckingham, 1982;

Clevedon Mercury archives, Clevedon;

Conway's *All the World's Fighting Ships 1860-1905,* Conway's Maritime publications;

Alfred S. Coulthard & Martin Watts, *Windmills of Somerset and the men who worked them;*

Valerie McNeill, *Mustads of Portishead.* Unpublished thesis, 1981. (Copy in Portishead Library);

National Nautical School. *Jubilee Year booklet,* N.N.S., 1954.

Paul Newman, *Channel Passage; the area round Portishead, Clevedon, Weston super Mare and Burnham on Sea,* Kingsmead Press, 1976;

Christopher Redwood, *Weston, Clevedon and Portishead Railway,* Sequoia Publishers, 1981;

Mike Vincent, *Reflections on the Portishead Branch,* Oxford Publishing Co., Poole, Dorset, 1983;

Eve Wigan, *Portishead Parish History,* Wessex Press, Taunton, 1932; *The Tale of Gordano,* Second Edition with additional notes by A.B.L. Reid, Chatford House Press, Bristol, 1971.

Portishead from Quarry.

H. B. & Son, Ltd., B

1. This view of the village was taken around the turn of the century from the site of the quarry off Newlands Hill, looking towards Portishead dock in which can be seen both sail and steam ships. At that time, the dock had only one quay, the side opposite being undeveloped – this view shows clearly the irregular shape of the original 'pill'. Lying off Portishead, in King Road, is the training ship H.M.S. *Formidable* which remained there at anchor from 1869 until 1906. According to census returns published in the *Clevedon Mercury* in 1903, the population of Portishead grew from 1,201 to 3,064 between 1861 and 1881, due to the construction of the docks and railway, but by 1901 it had fallen slightly to 2,539.

Portishead Church from N. W.

H. B. & Son. Ltd., B.

2. The founder of the first church at Portishead is unknown, and there is no mention of a church or chapel in the Domesday Book, but there was certainly a chapel in Norman times, signs of which were found, but unfortunately not preserved, during the 19th century 'restoration' work. The site of the Norman chapel is now covered by the vestry of the Parish Church. The bell tower was built in the 15th century by one of the groups or guilds of masons, each of which developed its own distinctive style of construction, using local stone. All the towers built by the group who constructed Portishead church tower have double buttresses, placed one on each side of the corners, but leaving the angle itself carrying its line straight up into the top pinnacles. The string courses are continued around the buttresses – the only Gloucestershire feature in a tower which is otherwise typically Somerset. This tower is more ornate than most of the others built by this N. Somerset group, and its parapet is pierced with a trefoil arcade. This photograph was taken before 1901 when the clock to commemorate Queen Victoria's Diamond Jubilee was installed, showing faces on three sides of the tower.

CROSS. PORTISHEAD CHURCH

3. Following the enclosure of Portishead between 1814 and 1823 whereby the common lands, open fields, homesteads, gardens and old enclosures were divided, allotted and enclosed, the public were given rights along various roads, bridleways and footpaths in the village. The former Mill Streete was widened to thirty feet from the old mill (now the 'White Lion') as far as Middle Bridge and was renamed High Street. It was probably about this time that the old village cross was removed from its site at the junction of Church Road South and Mill Streete to the churchyard where it stands today. The single stone which forms the shaft, some twelve feet high, may possibly have been a prehistoric 'mark-stone', such as are found along the tracks made by Stone Age folk.

ST. PETERS CHURCH, PORTISHEAD.

4. The Parish Church did not acquire its patron saint of St. Peter until the 19th century, which was also the period when it underwent significant structural alterations. The first of these were during the rectorship of Dr. John Shipton (1791-1838) who raised the floor and removed the old wooden screen which had once supported a roodloft above. Nothing of this now remains but the two sanctuary chairs inscribed by Dr. Shipton and his son John Nobel Shipton who was his curate. About 1880, the church was lengthened by moving the chancel eleven feet to the east, at the same time raising its arch by about four feet, and by inserting a new section of wall and a window. This view shows two of the Jubilee clock faces and also the former village cross which is now situated in the churchyard.

5. This interior view of St. Peter's Church was taken after the 1880 'restorations', when the wrought iron screen replaced the old oak one, but before 1910 when the wrought iron screen was itself removed and replaced by another oak screen. The wrought iron screen was transferred to St. Barnabas', West Hill (the 'iron church'), which was demolished in the 1970s. The font in the foreground was a replacement for the fine old Norman font which was thrown out during the 19th century. It in turn met with a similar fate, being removed during the alterations of the 1970s when the pews were taken out. The Norman font was found however, buried in a garden; it was rescued, restored to the church and now stands at the west end of the north aisle. The stone steps recessed in the wall, which now lead to the pulpit, formerly led to the roodloft which disappeared during the 19th century alterations. During the reconstruction, the floor level was also raised several feet, changing the proportions of the central stone arches and covering the gravestones set into the floor.

Parish Church, Court Farm & Roath Rd, Portishead, from the Air. 91333.

6. This aerial view taken during the mid-1920s shows St. Peter's in the centre and the buildings of Court Farm immediately below. To the left of Court Farm can be seen the old Rectory which had Elizabethan origins, was substantially extended during the nineteenth century but was demolished around 1970. High Street cuts across the lower right foreground and above it the houses in Roath Road lead up to Slade Road which runs along the top of the photograph. A similar view today would show that virtually the whole of the wooded and grassy area between Roath Road and Church Road North has disappeared and that the graves in the churchyard now extend all the way to Slade Road. St. Peter's Road now runs from the High Street to the junction of Slade Road, Church Road South and Newlands Hill.

7. Court Farm or Manor House was constructed during different periods. The lower half, now the farmhouse next to the fine barn, forms the original part and was probably built in Tudor days; the upper end, with its curious hexagonal tower faced at the corners with red brick, is Elizabethan. The tower contains just a winding staircase – its only purpose appears to be for the views obtainable from the larger seaward facing windows at the top which give excellent views of King Road and of the Channel west of Woodhill. For a time towards the end of the seventeenth century the tower end was converted into an inn, bearing 'The Tower House' as its sign. The City of Bristol began to buy up land in Portishead during the early seventeenth century, and in 1616 bought the manor of North Weston with its manor-house, now known as The Grange, and the manor of Portishead. Three years later, the City bought for £500 the Court or Manor House and its farm.

8. For this view of the High Street, the photographer was standing near the site of the present day Folk Hall, which in the 1880s was known as the Temperance Lecture Hall and in the late 1890s as the Salvation Army Hall. The road off to the right is Albert Road, and the large building standing on the corner behind the tree is the 'Victoria' public house, which was demolished in the late 1960s. The high wall on the left has gone, and on the land behind it there now stands a petrol filling station and garage. The cottages on the left have also disappeared – their site is presently occupied by the sheltered accommodation in Victoria Close. Apart from the two cyclists passing the horse-drawn delivery cart outside the 'Victoria', there are no other road users – just a few pedestrians. On the left hand side in the middle distance, the sign of the 'Anchor' hangs over the road unlike the 'Victoria' which does not appear to have a hanging sign.

9. This photograph of Portishead Fire Brigade (the name is just visible between the firemen's legs) was probably taken just after the arrival of the fire appliance in 1903. The Clevedon Mercury tells us that it arrived in Portishead on the 16th July that year and was kept in a shed prepared for it in the Council yard. Two days later at the Parish Wharf it was proudly exhibited under steam to the local residents. The 'Mercury' also informs us that the men of the newly formed Fire Brigade were to have the advantage of instruction from the Bristol Fire Brigade. On the right is another horse-drawn cart with some extending ladders in front of it. By 1904 it was reported that the fire crew consisted of A.H. Jenkins, Superintendent, G.W. Clarke, H.B. Coles, J. Tripp, F. Nesbitt, W.J. Small, W.J. Uncles and H. Woolford. Colonel De Cordes had been offered and had accepted the post of Captain.

The Anchor, Portishead.

10. Now called the 'Poacher', the 'Anchor' stands a little way back from the High Street. It is Portishead's oldest inn, having been known previously as the 'Gordon Arms' (at the time of the 1851 Census and in the 1855 Guide) and the 'Blew Anchor'. The inn was built in the 17th century, and at that time faced the village pond and green with its whipping post and stocks. The green most probably disappeared between 1814 and 1823 when the enclosure of Portishead was completed and the former Mill Streete was widened and renamed High Street, although it is interesting to note that the 1841 Census refers to it as Duck Street. The walled garden with its large tree has now gone and this area is now part of the forecourt of the 'Poacher'.

11. Portishead's Co-operative Society shops in the High Street flourished in earlier days, and provided a wide variety of services to the local community – the shops shown here were the drapery and the grocery. Daily deliveries of bread and groceries were made around the village by horse-drawn and hand-drawn carts. Due to competition from the supermarket chains, all have now ceased to trade in Portishead with the exception of the dairy which still provides a doorstep delivery service.

40717 Portishead, Old Cottage.

12. This lovely old thatched cottage stood in the High Street until it was pulled down to make way for the present Post Office building. In the late nineteenth century it was the home and business premises of Mr. Stephen Tuck who ran a car, a four-wheeled hackney carriage, to Bristol on Mondays, Thursdays and Saturdays at 8 o'clock for 8.30 a.m., returning from the 'Hope and Anchor' inn, Redcliff Hill, at 4 p.m.

HIGH ST. PORTISHEAD. (Looking South).

13. This postcard was sent in July 1907 and shows the view along the High Street from near the spot where Hartnell, Taylor & Cook premises stand today. The local Edwardian residents all appear to be smartly dressed in their Sunday best, posing for the photographer, and everybody in sight is wearing a hat – the ladies and girls in wide-brimmed hats and the men and boys in straw boaters or caps. The second shop on the right has been used for a variety of business over the years, and is presently Simper's toy shop; it was the first house in Portishead to have a telephone, and in this view displays a sign indicating that there is a telephone available for public use. The shop on the left, now Freeman's, was at that time a grocer's, displaying advertising signs in the windows. Although the road surface looks a little rough in this view, the message on the back of the card informs us that 'the roads are clean and well water'd'.

14. This card, posted in 1904, shows the proprietor and his family standing outside the shop and carries the message 'I send you a P.C. of old familiar faces'. A.T. Wilmott's butcher's shop and cottage have since been demolished – they stood just back from the High Street where Orchards and Barclays Bank trade today. The board below the shop window bears the message 'Shipping Supplied', most likely by means of the delivery horse and cart standing outside the shop. There appears to be some meat hanging outside by the door, a practice certainly not permitted by today's Public Health Authorities!

Portishead High Street

15. This tranquil scene looking along the High Street was taken just before the First World War. From the house behind the wall on the left Thomas Coles operated his daily carrier service to Bristol. His sign board spanned a side alley which led to the back yard where he kept his carts; the yard is used today by a local taxi service. This front wall was later taken down and some pumps were installed to provide a petrol filling station. On the right hand side, next to a hairdressers, was Portishead Post Office, then run by Mrs. Picton. Mr. Henry Bond ran Portishead's first Post Office in the building which we know today as the White Lion, along with his other business interests as a chemist, druggist and grocer. It was then moved to the shop which now trades as Fowler's the greengrocers, where it was run by the Pictons, before being transferred to the shop in this view. Post Office staff apparently worked long hours in the early 1900s, because the 'Clevedon Mercury' tells us that office hours were 7 a.m. to 8 p.m. weekdays; Sundays 8 a.m. to 10 a.m. There were four deliveries a day on weekdays and one letter delivery on Sundays.

High St. Portishead.

16. Taken from the corner of Stoke Road and the High Street on a fine summer day, judging from the small shadows being cast, this post-card view was sent in 1912. The only traffic in sight is a four wheeled Hackney carriage or fly apparently carrying a single passenger with a parasol. The pillared and arched front of the building on the right belongs to the National Provincial Bank of England which moved to these premises from the lower end of Nore Road (now known as Cabstand) in 1903 when this stone front extension was added. The bank now trades as the National Westminster Bank but has since demolished the extension in favour of a modern front. The fashionable hat of the day for men seems to be the straw boater.

17. Taken in June 1887 from the centre of the road, looking towards the church, the photographer has encouraged a cross-section of the local residents to pose for him around the Queen Victoria's Golden Jubilee arch erected across the road by the local builders Messrs. G. Biss & Sons. Through the arch, the shop on the left has a board which reads 'Portishead Grocery Supply – established for the Sale of Highest Class Teas, Coffees, Provisions & General Groceries at the Lowest Retail Prices for Ready Money Only. W.A. Hicks, Proprietor.' To the left of the arch is the shop of Mr. A. Wedmore, Seedsman, with its rows of watering cans hanging along the wall. The village celebrated the Jubilee over three days from the 21st to the 23rd June with many peals of bells from the parish church, special services at St. Peter's and churches of other denominations, an athletics meeting under A.A.A. rules on the cricket field at Tower Farm, a 'substantial meat tea' for some 900 working people in Mr. Tuck's paddock, another tea with sports and games for the 600 children of the parish and a large bonfire with fireworks organised by Dr. C. Wigan.

18. Taken on 24th May 1897, a large group of lads are standing in the High Street outside Frowd's Chemist's shop with its large bottles of coloured liquids in the window; the shop bears the date 1891 and is still a chemist's today, now trading as Drummond's. Many of the lads appear to be working lads – there is one in apron, one with a bread basket and one with a delivery barrow. In addition to being a chemist's shop, Frowd's appears to have sold newspapers, the 'Times & Mirror', the 'Bristol Mercury' and the 'Western Daily Press' being prominently advertised outside. We know that the photograph was taken on that date because the 'Times & Mirror' placard includes the headlines 'Funeral of Lord Edward Somerset', and 'Blackwall Tunnel Opening by Prince of Wales'. The next shop along is Osmond the draper, and next door again is W.O. Cole. Beyond W.O. Cole is G.W. Clarke, family grocer, and then Wedmore, seedsman before we come to Major, tailors & outfitters. In the distance, on the right, is A.T. Wilmott, family butcher, whose shop is shown in closer detail at No. 14 in this book, just in front of the thatched cottage which was demolished to make way for the present day Post Office.

19. Shop fronts, cars and fashions change over the years, but the upper floors and roofs of buildings of today's High Street show little difference since this postcard was sent in 1922. Osmond's shop on the left is still trading (now as Osmond and Tovey), and Lloyds Bank still conducts business at the premises on the corner of the High Street and Combe Road. Children can, however, no longer stand and play in the middle of the road, due to the growth in traffic, but the general scene has changed very little. The sight of a motor car in the High Street was apparently not unusual at the time when this photograph was taken – the passage of this car has aroused very little interest from the majority of folk.

Combe Road, Portishead.

20. Combe Road was built around the turn of the century to connect the High Street with Slade Road, built somewhat earlier. The house on the left bears the date 1899 and is today the offices of a local firm of solicitors. This card was posted in 1906, when the house was occupied by G. Biss whose signboard describes him as being 'Carpenter, Builder and Undertaker'. The first house on the right was then occupied by Mr. E.O. Major, outfitter, who apparently moved to these premises when they were built. Mr. Major's previous premises were in the High Street, as mentioned in the caption to the 1897 view at No. 18. Combe Road ended at its junction with Slade Road – Avon Way was not built until the late 1960s. The houses visible on the skyline in the distance are on West Hill and could be reached from Combe Road by a footpath up Dry Hill.

SLADE ROAD PORTISHEAD

21. Slade Road is one of Portishead's oldest roads, and in the nineteenth century was known as Slade Lane. It became an important route because it linked the main part of the original village, clustered around the church, with the fort on Battery Point via its continuation known today as Battery Lane. This view, dating from around 1918, is taken from the corner of Combe Road with Slade Road, looking towards Battery Point; the terrace of houses on the left were the first to be built along Slade Road away from the church area. The trees have since disappeared, and houses now run the full length of the road on both sides.

WHITE LION HOTEL, PORTISHEAD.

22. The White Lion Hotel, formerly known as the Old Mill, appears on the earliest maps of Portishead. It was a flour mill driven by an undershot wheel, and stood astride the Portishead Pill or Yeo which drained the Gordano valley and flowed into Portishead pill. The arch across the water can be seen in the lower right hand corner of this view, taken from where the Somerset Hall stands today. The large tree on the left is still standing there today, but the rest of this attractive garden has disappeared under the tarmac of the White Lion car park. During the eighteenth century, this fresh water mill was converted to a tide mill by the construction of a dam to impound the high tides, but this caused drainage problems in the surrounding moorlands. Following the 1810 Act 'for draining and improving lands in the manors or parishes of North Weston, Walton, etc.,' the City dismantled the mill and partly rebuilt it, letting it as a private house.

PORTISHEAD. HIGH STREET. 65540

23. It is difficult for the present day resident of Portishead to imagine how at high tide the water in the pill used to reach as far as the old mill just visible at the left hand edge of this view. This allowed the local lads to dive off its wall into the water, and also enabled barges to sail right up to it. Even today it is possible to see an iron ring, reputedly used for tying up boats, set into the wall opposite, the location of the old parish wharf. The Portishead Methodists of 1884 met in a house with an annexe in the Newtown district of Portishead; it is now a private dwelling house – 39 Albert Road. The foundation stones of the present Methodist Church on the right of this view were laid on 28th September 1886 and in the following year on 24th May it was opened and dedicated for public worship. One day in the future, some inhabitants of Portishead will find under the first stone a bottle containing 1886 editions of the 'Methodist Recorder', the 'Methodist Times', the 'Joyful News' and the 'Clevedon Mercury', together with a programme of the day's proceedings, a poster, a plan of the building and a list of the Trustees.

Weston and Clevedon Light Railway Terminus, Portishead

24. Although Portishead is now without a passenger train service, between the years 1907 to 1940 it was served by two quite different railway systems. While the Great Western Railway provided a link with Bristol, the Weston, Clevedon and Portishead Light Railway gave travellers a direct connection between these resorts. The line was first proposed in an unsuccessful Act of Parliament in 1865, but authority was subsequently given by the Weston-super-Mare, Clevedon and Portishead Tramways Act of 1885. It was 1897 before the first train ran between Weston and Clevedon, and another decade before the line to Portishead was opened. The terminus at Portishead was a simple structure, comprising a waiting room, booking office and a ladies' room, and was reached from the High Street along the lane which passed under the arch of the White Lion. The level crossing across the lane linked the W.C. & P.L.R. with the G.W.R. track, but its overgrown state shows that there were no through services. The Light Railway went into decline during the 1930s and after a succession of years with mounting operational losses, the line was finally closed on 18th May 1940.

OUR LOCAL EXPRESS
Clevedon to Portishead

25. The Weston, Clevedon and Portishead Light Railway was not known for extravagance, and operated a motley collection of second-hand locomotives and rolling stock, although not quite as basic as the postcard sent in 1908 depicts! Nor was its service renowned for its speed, because a glance at a timetable shows that a journey from Portishead to Clevedon took between twenty-five and thirty-five minutes, calling at six stations on the way, to say nothing of the need for the crew to stop the train at every level crossing to open and close the gates – crossing keepers were unknown on this line. Such a railway was bound to attract tales, some no doubt apocryphal, such as the one about the fireman who stopped his train to pick some particularly juicy mushrooms from a field alongside the line, and then proceeded to fry them on his shovel! Another alleged that the W.C. & P. trains carried cow-catchers at the rear to prevent damage from overtaking cattle! It is also claimed that a handwritten notice on one of the waiting shelters read 'Passengers are requested not to pick blackberries while the train is in motion'.

26. As the road name on the side of the building shows, B. Warren's shop stood on the corner of Ferndale Road and the High Street in the early years of the century. Prior to the Warrens, it was occupied by E. Mitchell, fishmonger and fruiterer. In addition to selling the Cadbury's and Fry's products advertised in the window, the Misses Warren standing outside the shop also offered a comprehensive range of services, the most prominently advertised being their agency for Brooks Dye works in Bristol. Other signs in the window show that they served 'Teas' and 'Refreshments', and the notice propped up on the wall states 'Wash and Brush-up' 2d. The plaque to the left of the window advertises that Gilbert Warren, sculptor, could be contacted through the shop, and a sign in the garden reads 'Cycles stored', presumably for the benefit of cycling visitors to Portishead wishing to view the village and surroundings on foot. In the background, the roof of the present day library can be seen, a building which has previously served Portishead as Assembly Rooms and as a cinema.

HIGH ST. PORTISHEAD (LOOKING SOUTH)

27. This card was posted in 1906 and shows a view of the High Street taken from its junction with the bottom end of Nore Road (now called Cabstand), looking towards the White Lion. The wall on the left has now gone as has the structure resembling a shelter – today it is a wide expanse of roadway, the first part of Portishead reached by visitors arriving via Wyndham Way. The two young ladies with their dolls and perambulator are playing outside the café at 3 Litfield Buildings which was then run by Mr. and Mrs. Thomas, and just past it can be seen some posters advertising some coming attractions in the Assembly Rooms, in use today as the Portishead branch of the Avon County Library.

From the Air.9133?

28. The building in the immediate foreground of this aerial view is that of the Portishead and District Electric Light and Power Company, reached by a road off the High Street which passed through the White Lion. Though now filled in, the arch is still visible today. This road also led to the terminus of the Weston, Clevedon and Portishead Light Railway which can be seen just above the Electricity Company building. The present Wyndham Way is constructed along the line of the old track leading away to the left of this view. There was a track over a level crossing connecting the Light Railway to the Great Western Railway line to Bristol, but no passenger trains ran through. Across the High Street from the White Lion stands the Wesleyan Chapel and to its right the Infant School which bears the date 1840. On the corner of Ferndale Road and the High Street can be seen the shop described at No. 26 of this book. Slade Road shows clearly along the top of the photograph overlooking a large open expanse of grass and trees, and is connected to the High Street by Combe Road in the centre of this view.

29. During the nineteenth century when the use of horse transport was at its height, horseshoe nails were still made by hand; although ordinary nails had been made by machines for some time, the special techniques for manufacturing horseshoe nails by machine proved difficult and it was not until the turn of the century that a Norwegian named Clarin Mustad perfected the process that had defeated machinery engineers for so long. For a few years, Mustad's machine-made nails were distributed by their agent Mr. F. Burris of Bristol, but they then decided to set up a factory in England. Portishead was chosen because of its good dock, rail and road connections and a three acre site was purchased from Bristol Corporation in Gas House Lane, now called Old Mill Lane. Mustads sent over a number of Scandinavian staff to supervise the construction of the factory, and commenced production in 1911 using local labour – Portishead's first industry. At that time there were some eight other companies in England making horseshoe nails, but Mustads began to buy them up in order to obtain their markets and trade names. By 1926, only the Capewell Horse Nail Company at Leicester was left. Mustads took over Capewells in 1928, and thus became the sole manufacturer of horseshoe nails in Britain until the factory was closed down in 1987.

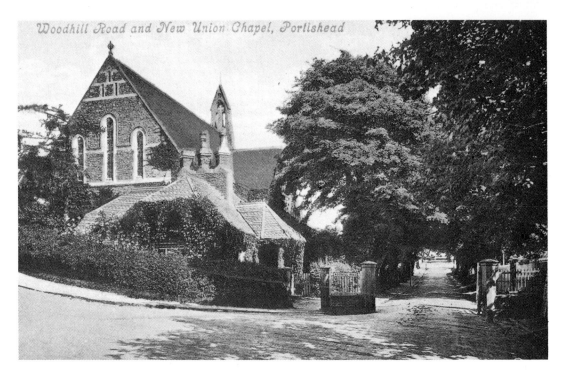

Woodhill Road and New Union Chapel, Portishead

30. When the Corporation of Bristol started to develop Portishead as a seaside resort in the 1820s, they constructed a drive, the first part flanked by sycamore trees, from Nore Road up Woodhill as far as the landing stage. At its junction with Nore Road, a gatehouse was built in 1828 to house a toll-keeper, and a gate was hung across Woodhill Road. When this photograph was taken around the turn of the century, the gate posts and gate were still in position. The earliest records of Congregational witness in Portishead show that a Mrs. Waterman held a service in her home on 6th March 1840. She then generously provided a plot of land for a permanent building which was to become known as the Chapel on the Hill. It was built with financial assistance from 'Five Gentlemen of Bristol', and was opened for public worship on 16th September 1840. The Church prospered, and by 1875 the need for increased accommodation led to a search for a more suitable piece of land. This was obtained at the junction of Nore Road and Battery Road, and the foundation stone of the new Union Church was laid on 9th December 1875 by Mr. W.H. Wills, M.P., later Lord Winterstoke.

PORTISHEAD. BATTERY ROAD.

31. This postcard shows another view of the Union Church looking along Battery Road from Beach Road, and was taken around 1910. Designed in the early Gothic style, Victorian craftsmen took only sixteen months to build it, the first service being held on 24th April 1877. Not long after the opening, a magnificent organ was installed – it was bought for £200 'from the old jail by the new cut' in Bristol. It was subsequently called the Union Congregational Church, but is today known as the United Reformed Church. The field on the right was at that time used for the Portishead Flower Show.

32. The first houses in Adelaide Terrace date from 1850, the time when the Corporation of Bristol started to spend considerable sums of money on its estates in Portishead to attract visitors and new residents. The first seven are built in local stone and have ornamental gables, unlike those further along which were constructed a little later in dressed Bath stone, with fanlights above the doors. The first resident at number one was the redoubtable Honourable Caroline Boyle, former lady-in-waiting to Queen Adelaide, consort of William IV, after whom the terrace was named. She was a speaker of great conviction, and preached many a sermon in the Temperance Hall, now the Folk Hall, when she was not driving around in a landau, urging villagers to repent. At number ten, according to the Bond and Fardon Guide to Portishead of 1855, lived Mr. Henry Pick from whom visitors were encouraged to hire a 'safe and commodious sailing boat' for a trip around the bay.

Adelaide Terrace, Portishead

33. A view of the back of Adelaide Terrace, looking towards Woodhill, is shown on this card posted in 1908. When they were built, many of the houses were given elegant wrought iron balconies such as can be seen along the Georgian terraces in Clifton, but a century and a half of salt laden sea air has done irreparable damage, and relatively few are remaining today. The twin gabled house on the right is today known as 'The Abbey', but when this photograph was taken it was called 'Hillside', the family home of the Weatherlys; visible above the terrace is 'Fircliff', and just above it the roof of 'The Gnoll' (demolished in 1985) peeps through the trees. Battery Lane runs behind the Terrace and Beach Road crosses the foreground; the greenhouses belonged to Mr. Fowler who had his nursery there at that time – they were subsequently demolished when Rodmoor Road was built.

Photo by Herbert Lambert, Bath

Fred. E. Weatherly

34. Fred. E. Weatherly K.C. was born in 1848 and brought up at 'Hillside', now called 'The Abbey', in Woodhill Road, Portishead, one of thirteen children born to Dr. Frederick Weatherly, known as the 'Grand Old Man of North Somerset', who practised medicine in the village and surrounding area for over sixty years until he was ninety. Fred. E. Weatherly was educated at Hereford School and studied at Brasenose College, Oxford, before becoming a barrister, but he always retained a great interest in ships, books and music, developed during his early years at Portishead. Known as 'The People's Laureate', he wrote verse, translated operas into english and wrote the lyrics for some 1,500 Victorian songs and ballads. Probably the best remembered of his words are those written for 'The Holy City', 'Roses of Picardy', 'Green Hills of Somerset' and 'Danny Boy'.

35. Taken in the mid-1920s from the air, this photograph takes in the view from South Avenue, running across the foreground to the Marine Lake at the top. Apart from the Police Station just visible at the foot of the photograph, there were no houses along South Avenue which then formed one side of a field, bounded on its two other sides by Woodhill Road and Beach Road; when this view was taken, the field was being grazed by some cattle. The long line of Adelaide Terrace shows clearly, and beyond it is the Marine Drive, now known as Lake Road; Rodmoor Road connecting Beach Road with the Marine Drive was built later. The newly laid road at right centre is Gardner Road.

RAILWAY STATION, PORTISHEAD

36. In 1863, the Bristol & Portishead Pier and Railway Company received the Royal assent to the Act of Parliament authorising the construction of a pier at Portishead and a railway from that pier to the Bristol & Exeter Railway at Bedminster. It was originally a single line broad gauge track and was opened on 18th April 1867. These handsome buildings stood on the land just inside the present entrance gates to the Central Electricity Generating Board's Power Station site, but were demolished in 1955 in order to create access to the site on which Portishead 'B' Power Station was to be built. A new station was built about half a mile away to the south involving in turn the demolition of the local Labour Exchange, a British Legion hut, a Boy Scouts' headquarters, a blacksmith's forge and a jeweller's shop, and came into service on 4th January 1954. The life of the new passenger station proved to be a brief one, because the branch line fell victim to the Beeching cuts of the 1960s and closed to passengers on 5th September 1964. The new station buildings were subsequently converted into a petrol filling station and car showroom.

Portishead Railway Station. 423.

37. This postcard view of Portishead's Great Western Railway Station was taken from the footbridge across the tracks during the 1920s. Having been originally constructed as a broad gauge railway by the Bristol & Portishead Pier and Railway Company, it was converted to standard gauge in January 1880; four years later it was vested in the GWR, who by then had taken over the Bristol & Exeter Railway, by means of the GWR & Portishead Railway Act of 1884. Taken on a hazy day, this view looks in the direction of the pier station, the tall chimney of Bailey's mill being just discernible in the distance. The building on the right is the engine shed.

RAILWAY STATION, PORTISHEAD.

38. This postcard provides another view of the old Great Western Railway Station buildings at Portishead and was taken around 1910. Passengers arriving could take one of the Hackney carriages standing outside the station into the village away to the right. At that time, the Seamen's Institute stood in Station Road close to the railway station, almost opposite the point where the present Beach Road West joins it. Station Road ended at this point, but there was a footpath for pedestrians leading towards the Royal Hotel and Chesil beach beyond.

Railway Station. Portishead. 599.

39. A different view of Portishead's Great Western Railway Station and goods sidings, looking towards the village, taken during the 1920s. Behind the building in the foreground is an engine turntable; the station buildings are on the right in the distance, just in front of the footbridge. Beyond the ship in the dock the chimney of Mustad's horseshoe nail factory is visible, and the tree and grass covered slope of Portishead Down above the village is as yet undeveloped. The footpath on the right leading straight towards the photographer runs between the end of Station Road and the Royal Hotel.

THE DOCK PORTISHEAD. 91.

"WRIGHTS PICTURES"

40. Portishead dock was constructed by widening and impounding the tidal 'pill', and apart from the construction of a wall along the east side of the dock this century to serve as a timber wharf, seen in the background of this view, the dock today is largely in its original state. Much of the old 'pill' was filled in with ashes from the Power Station, so that it is no longer possible to see its original size and shape, but the old right of way running from the sea wall past the new parish wharf to the old tide mill, now the White Lion, still exists. The viaduct across the dock carried the railway track to Portishead station – to the left of this photograph, just out of view. The rails visible on the left connected the Great Western line to that of the Weston, Clevedon and Portishead Light Railway. This postcard view was taken around 1914 when steam ships outnumbered sailing ships in the dock.

The Docks, Portishead

41. The construction of docks at Portishead and Avonmouth during the 1870s resulted from problems encountered in Bristol City docks due to growth in traffic and the increasing size of ships. The work also stemmed from an intense rivalry between the Bristol Port Railway & Pier Company, which built a pier at Avonmouth and a railway connection to Hotwells in 1864-65, and the Bristol and Portishead Pier & Railway Company, who opened a broad gauge line to Portishead in 1867 and completed the pier in 1870. Both companies obtained authorising Acts of Parliament for the construction of their respective docks, but Portishead suffered from constructional delays and the dock was not completed until 1879, some two years after Avonmouth. The first ship to enter the dock was the company's own pleasure steamer Lyn followed a week later by the first cargo boat – the Magdeburg from Galatz, laden with barley. This view was taken around 1920 from the north-east corner of the dock looking towards the village, with Portishead Down in the background. On the left can be seen the cranes on the timber wharf.

H.M.S.HUSSAR PORTISHEAD

42. The odd-looking ship in this postcard, with its two funnels very far apart, probably visited Portishead round about the time of the First World War and is classed as a torpedo gunboat, armed with five torpedo tubes and seven guns. H.M.S. Hussar was constructed at Devonport dockyard in 1893-1895, converted to a minesweeper in 1914 and was broken up in 1921.

ROYAL TERRACE, PORTISHEAD.   *will + place all when possible*   HB&S

43. This fine stone-built terrace was built around 1880 just off Pier Road with a short cul-de-sac (now part of Leigh View Road) in front of the six houses. They stood in splendid isolation for many decades, surrounded by grass and trees, but during the 1960s, the four nearest the camera were demolished leaving just the pair which still stand there today, now hemmed in by modern houses and looking out across the Power Stations and Docks.

Entrance to Pier, PORTISHEAD.

44. Horse-drawn hackney carriages known as 'flys' or 'cars' used to wait by the entrance to the Royal Hotel to meet visitors arriving at Portishead pier, to convey them to their destinations or to take them on a horse-drawn tour of the village. This view was taken around the turn of the century, looking towards Avonmouth, and shows a Campbell's steamer leaving the pier with the 'Formidable' moored in the background.

45. In the 1820s, the Corporation of Bristol, who were owners of much of the land at Portishead, are said to have spent over £20,000 in development of amenities to attract people here – the Royal Hotel was probably the only seaside hotel built by a public authority in Britain during the nineteenth century. Construction commenced in 1829 in accordance with plans drawn up by Mr. Geo. Dymond, a Bristol architect – it was described in the 1842 Portishead Guide as being Gothic in style. It opened for business in 1831 under the management of Miss Pring; she was still there twenty years later when she had a staff consisting of a vintner James Wait, three female servants, one male servant, an ostler and a tap boy. The Corporation has since disposed of the freehold, but the Royal Hotel remains a symbol of public enterprise at a time when private enterprise was the norm. This card was posted in 1910, and was probably offered for sale at the hotel, because, unlike most other cards in this book, it bears no postcard publisher's name.

The Pier, Portishead.

46. After completion of the Royal Hotel, Bristol Corporation built a small landing slipway just below the hotel to encourage visitors to this seaside resort. In 1839, Brunel put forward proposals for a pier at Portishead with road connections to Bristol, to make it easier for passengers to join his newest engineering creation, the Great Western, for the onward journey to New York; this plan also included a road bridging the 'pill' to enable easy access to the Royal Hotel for transatlantic passengers. This was succeeded by another Brunel scheme in 1845 proposing the construction of Portbury floating pier, landing place and steam packet harbour with rail connections to Bristol in continuation of the line of the Great Western Railway. Nothing unfortunately came of these grand designs, but a small stone pier was finally built in 1849 to enable trippers to disembark just below the Royal Hotel. In 1870 it was extended by the Bristol and Portishead Pier & Railway Company. This photograph, taken from the grounds of the Royal Hotel, shows some Edwardian ladies enjoying the view of the pier and shipping in King Road.

THE PIER, PORTISHEAD. NO.2.   HB&S

47. Taken around the turn of the century, this postcard shows a few local inhabitants or visitors leaning on the posts of Portishead pier engaged in the ever popular pastime of watching the shipping in King Road (except at this particular moment when they were watching the photographer). The 'Formidable' lies at anchor, close to shore, and more sailing ships are in the distance, sailing to or from Avonmouth and Bristol.

Portishead. H.M.S. Formidable

48. In 1869, two Bristol citizens – Henry Fedden and Augustine Woodward – became so concerned about the 'street arabs' (urchins from poor and deprived homes in need of care and protection) that they arranged a meeting, chaired by the Mayor of Bristol, which resolved to ask the Lords of the Admiralty to loan them an old warship to moor in the River Severn as a training ship for such boys. The Bristol Training Ship was to be an Industrial School Ship to give nautical training which would fit the boys for service in the Royal or Merchant Navies. The Admiralty leased the sponsors H.M.S. Formidable, a 2,289 ton 2-decker built at Chatham in 1825 and originally fitted with 84 guns, which had been serving as a flagship moored off Sheerness from 1860 to 1868, her armament by then having been reduced to 26 guns. Late in 1869 she was towed to Portishead and moored 400 yards off shore. The cost of repairs, adaptation and towing was about £3,000, raised by voluntary subscriptions given in response to an appeal made by Mr. Fedden. The first boy was received on board on 1st December 1869, the opening ceremony being performed by the Reverend Charles Kingsley.

No. 969. The Formidable in her last days.   "A. C. & Co." Series.

49. For nearly forty years the Formidable remained a well-known feature of Portishead's maritime scene, and during that time over 3,500 boys were taken on board and trained. By the end of the last century however, serious problems were becoming apparent in the 75 year old ship. It necessitated the stepping of new wooden masts in 1898, and work to stop the hull leaks which were developing due to the deterioration of her copper sheathing and of the caulking in her seams. Matters came to a head in 1900 after she was damaged in a severe gale, and about that time opinions began to turn in favour of shore training establishments. The Inspectors of Schools were emphatically in favour that the school should move ashore, and Edward Gabriel was engaged to draw up plans for the National Nautical School. The site was ready for the ceremonial laying of the foundation stone in 1904, and the 350 boys moved to their new building in January 1906. Shortly afterwards, the 'Formidable' was towed away to be broken up.

Portishead,from the Air.91543.

50. This aerial view of Woodhill, looking towards Battery Point, was taken in the mid-1920s, probably on the same day as No. 6 in this book – the Royal Hotel shows up clearly with its circular drive leading to the main entrance. The buildings just below it to the left are Dock House, Pier Cottage and the old Pier station at the end of the Great Western Railway's Bristol to Portishead branch line. Pier Road on the left leads towards Royal Terrace facing an open expanse of green, unlike its present day view of Portishead 'B' Power Station. Broad Walk can be seen through the midst of the trees covering Woodhill, and just visible on the right, above the rocky shore of Chesil beach, are some of the large houses along Woodlands Road.

The Beach, Portishead.

51. Chesil beach was popular for many years, being the nearest to Portishead's railway stations; it was reached by steps leading down from the grounds of the Royal Hotel. This card posted in 1913 shows that the beach was far from sandy, but that did not seem to deter the day trippers. It was shut off from the dock by the projecting headland and the Bristol Mercury Guide describes it as being 'a most inviting sheltered and secluded nook, backed by luxuriant foliage which slopes down to the pebbles of the beach'. Boats and skiffs were available during the summer season for a sail or a row down the coast past the Battery.

The Broad Walk, Portishead 270/3

52. The Bristol Mercury Guide to Portishead of 1884 describes the Broad Walk across the top of Woodhill as 'most inviting, with ample means of resting or pic-nicing in the midst of leafy woods and in view of the sea'. It was created by the Corporation of Bristol at the time that they constructed Woodhill Road and the road leading to the Royal Hotel, as one of the attractions for visitors to Portishead. It is not so well-maintained today, being somewhat overgrown and narrower. The Guide also tells us that when the dense undergrowth was re-moved, well-defined traces of an old camp were revealed, situated on the north side of the hill and enclosing a considerable piece of ground sloping from the summit of the hill to the shore. It formed an irregular rhomboid, its longest diameter being about four hundred yards, and its shortest two hundred yards. The south-western angle was at the end of the broad glade at the summit of the woods.

Woodlands Road. Portishead.

53. During the early nineteenth century, some fine residences were built along Woodlands Road – this view looking towards the Royal Hotel shows 'Eastwood' which enjoys fine views across the Bristol Channel to Wales and northwards to the Cotswolds. It was constructed by Mr. S. Dawkes, architect, of Gloucester, and its grounds 'graced by a beautiful group of parterres, plats of floral rarities, gardens and shady walks' were designed by James Tanner, the bailiff of the Bristol Corporation's property at Portishead. Further along Woodlands Road, between 'Eastwood' and Battery Point, stood the Baths and Reading Room, built during the 1830s; the site is now occupied by the house known as 'The Saltings'. Bond and Fardon's New Portishead Guide of 1855 described the baths as a 'classical little structure' in which were housed 'hot, cold and plunging baths, dressing rooms and saloons, with a singular contrivance by which the discoloured waters of the Channel are converted, by filtration, into a perfectly limpid element, without losing a grain of their saline impregnation'. They had a short life however, and appear to have closed down during the 1860s.

The Esplanade, Portishead.

54. Taken not long after it was opened in 1898, this photograph shows Portishead's new esplanade with a Victorian mother taking her children for a walk along it – the lady behind her holding the perambulator is probably the nursemaid. The plans for a promenade to link Beach Road with Battery Point (with the sanction of the War Office) were first drawn up in 1882 – the scheme involved raising the level of the existing path and banking it with turf, but because insufficient funds were available and due to it not receiving the approval of the Lord of the Manor, the plans were dropped. A great gale in the winter of 1883/84 banked up tons of huge stones and boulders, reducing the amount of work to be done, but work did not commence until several years later. The Clevedon Mercury tells us that the shelter on the esplanade was erected as 'the permanent memorial from the grateful people of Portishead of their much beloved Queen Victoria', in celebration of her Diamond Jubilee in 1897.

THE MARINE LAKE, PORTISHEAD.

WRIGHT'S "ARTISTIC" SERIES

55. Taken just after its completion in 1910, this rural scene with cows in the foreground shows the new Marine Lake, sheltering behind the protective bank of the esplanade. Designed by Bristolian Peter Addie, the lake and surrounding pleasure grounds were the result of an ambitious scheme promoted by Bristol Corporation both to improve the attractions of Portishead and to create work for Bristol's unemployed. The lake was dug out by hand from what were previously the withy beds, thorny brushwood and stagnant rhynes of low-lying Rodmoor, of interest only to local children as an 'adventure playground', and to skaters on the rare occasions when the flooded moor froze over in winter. A swan hut was built on the island in the lake, and many families of cygnets have been successfully raised there over the years.

Marine Lake, Portishead

56. The Marine Lake and pleasure grounds soon became a major attraction for visitors to Portishead as can be seen in this view taken around the time of the First World War. Boating was a popular way to spend an hour on a sunny summer afternoon, but if that was considered too energetic, there was always the alternative of sitting around in deck chairs under parasols or sun hats – suntans were not then in fashion. Although the lake was not deep enough to swim in, bathing was apparently allowed, judging from the changing cubicles to be seen on the far side of the lake.

57. This view of the new esplanade looking down the end of Beach Road (West) towards Battery Point was taken around 1900 before Beach Villas were built; the beach then looked cleaner and more attractive than it does today with sea grass growing over the mud flats. Because of its commanding position overlooking the main sea approach to Bristol, the Point was one of the City's recognised defence points and it is recorded that a watch tower stood there in Elizabethan times when Spain threatened; the first major development took place however in the mid-seventeenth century during the Civil War when Portishead Fort, as it was then known, was defended by a garrison of local Cavaliers. Local history records that in 1685 the Point was honoured with a visit by King James II, accompanied by Prince George of Denmark and attended by many noblemen. The Battery was refortified during Napoleonic times and again during the two world wars for anti-submarine defence purposes, but since then the Point has been fully open to the public, and today virtually no trace remains of the old fortifications. The open-air swimming pool was built in 1962.

BEACH & HILL, PORTISHEAD.   HB&S

58. Although this postcard dates from around 1902, this view taken from Nore Road looking towards Battery Point is somewhat older, having been taken before the esplanade was completed in 1898. At that time there was just a footpath between the Point and Beach Road (West), and only the ridge of shingle stood between the high tides and the low-lying area of Rodmoor. It is recorded that the house which stands prominently on the Point was occupied by the caretaker of the fort. When Battery Point was owned by the War Office, Woodhill Bay was used as a rifle range. The targets were set up on the rocky promontory beside protective shelters built to house the target spotters. These shelters were shaped like half cylinders and when the firing ceased, the spotters would signal the hits using a system of flags. Firing points were located along the beach at distances of 300, 500 and 600 yards.

HOTEL COMO, PORTISHEAD.

59. This fine Georgian residence was known as Como House during the nineteenth century, and was used as a private house until 1897 when it was bought by Mr. Edwin Lloyd, 'a well-known and influential London gentleman', with the intention of converting it to a high class boarding house. Later that year, he applied for a license after spending some £5,000 on furnishing and improvement, but it was not granted due to opposition from the Temperance Society, who presented a petition, and from the police who considered that the place was over-run with public houses – there was one for every 278 persons in the village! Mr. Lloyd re-applied the following year, and was successful on that occasion. Now known as the Bay Hotel, the Hotel Como was described in 1899 as one of the most luxuriously appointed hotels in the kingdom. This view shows the elegant stone balustrade of the Italian Terrace, which today has unfortunately disappeared and has been replaced by the tarmac of the hotel car park. It then enjoyed over three acres of private grounds, including a nuttery, and residents could either relax with a quiet stroll or could be more energetic and indulge in a game of tennis or croquet.

Wood Hill, from Golf Links, Portishead.

60. Local records around the turn of the century tell us that Portishead had a golf links off Gas House Road, now Old Mill Lane, but in 1908 Harry Vardon laid out the golf links shown on this postcard. The course was a full eighteen holes, just over 5,000 yards long, and extended over 82 acres of Portishead Down, both above and below Nore Road. Mr. Ashford, the green keeper for forty years, lived on Nore Road in Fern Cottage, demolished a few years before the Mariners Park estate was built. After the Second World War, the golf club closed, but Portishead today still has an eighteen hole approach course run by the District Council and mown by mechanical means rather than the more natural method seen in this photograph.

GOLF CLUB HOUSE, PORTISHEAD.

61. The Golf Club House was built in 1908, incorporating the disused tower of Portishead windmill, clearly seen in this view, which ceased operations in the mid-1840s. The course was far from easy, being constructed on both sides of Nore Road along the slope of Portishead Down, and during the following thirty years was dug up twice in both world wars to assist food supplies with crops of corn and potatoes. These factors together with the competition from other local courses brought about its closure, and the former club premises are now used as the Hole in One public house and restaurant. Underneath the present day car park between the Hole in One and Nore Road (originally known as Washing Pool Drove), lies the nineteenth century washing pool for sheep, which was fed by a stream from the Down above. This stream has today been largely covered over, but can still be seen running down the hill below the Hole in One.

Sept. 1919.

THE BATHING BEACH, PORTISHEAD — E.H.W.

62. Although the beaches at Portishead were not really suited to bathing, the Council received a request in the 1890s to provide suitable facilities for ladies. It was accordingly agreed to lease sixty perches of land for this purpose in Sheepwash Bay below the site of the old windmill along Nore Road – this was subsequently known as the Ladies' Bathing Beach. Screens were erected and an attendant was employed to guard the beach when ladies in serge bloomers were using it. The safe bathing area, about two feet deep at high tide, was marked with posts and chains which can be seen at the left of this photograph.

THE NORE ROAD, PORTISHEAD.

HB&S

63. Probably taken during the 1890s, this view along Nore Road shows clearly the remains at that time of Portishead windmill. It was one of the last built in Somerset, being finished in 1832, according to an indenture made between the City of Bristol and John Nesbitt, miller, on 25th March that year. The indenture records that the stone tower mill and cottage were 'completed according to a plan and elevation already submitted by the said John Nesbitt to the Surveyors of City Lands'. It had one of the shortest working lives of any mill because by 1846 John Nesbitt had left the mill and no new tenant could be found. Permission was sought in 1848 to remove the mill machinery and convert the tower into a dwelling to provide additional accommodation for the tenant of the mill cottage which lies a little way further down the hill, just out of sight in this postcard. According to a legal letter dated 4th May 1848, the failure was 'in consequence of there being a mill in Portishead worked by steam'. The mill store can be seen adjacent to the mill tower in this photograph, but later photographs taken just after 1900 show just the tower capped with a pointed roof.

Nore Avenue, Portishead.

64. Taken in the early years of this century, this view of Nore Road was taken from around the point where the present day Raleigh Rise joins it, looking towards Redcliffe Bay. This stretch of Nore Road was known as The Avenue or Nore Avenue, being in those days a shady country road lined with tall trees, planted by a benefactor unknown, and ended just short of where the Nautical School now stands. It thus provided a quiet level stretch of road along which perambulators could be easily pushed, as is being done in this view. Then, as nowadays, visitors to Portishead found the coastal views and spectacular summer sunsets over the Welsh hills a great attraction. Today, unfortunately, there are very few of these trees left, most having been felled for safety reasons, and the volume of traffic along Nore Road has destroyed its former tranquillity.

The Loaf of Bread
& Bay Portishead

65. The beach commonly known today as Sugar Loaf Beach was previously known as the Loaf of Bread, apparently a reference to the large square shaped rock situated at the end of it. It was a popular beach, although when this photograph was taken around 1917 there were only a few visitors – some appear to have brought their own changing tent with them. As an additional attraction, the Urban District Council later provided a diving platform and a raft for swimmers; subsequent improvements included changing cubicles and a children's pool, refilled by each high tide. Today, relatively few people use the Loaf beach for bathing – the main users are now Portishead Yacht and Sailing Club which is based there.

66. Nore Farm dates from 1701, and from 1845 until 1953 it was owned and farmed by four generations of the Ashford family. The first of these was John Ashford, who bought the farm in 1845 from Thomas Wilmott, followed by Joseph, James and lastly Jim who retired from farming in 1953. Most of the land previously farmed by the Ashfords is now covered by housing and the Nautical School, but Nore Farm still has one field attached to it, sloping down towards the Channel, occupied by a variety of birds and animals. The Ashfords at one time farmed some eighty acres of Portishead – a mixture of dairy and arable farming, and supplemented their income with market gardening in the summer and with fishing for sprats during the winter, using nets staked out in the Channel which were emptied at each low tide, as is still done in Bridgwater Bay today. A good catch used to yield seven or eight hundredweight, which was then sold for fourpence a pound from a horse and cart driven around Portishead, Portbury and Pill, and sometimes was taken into St. Nicholas fish market in Bristol. Catches declined due to the growth of pollution in the Channel, and stake-net fishing at Portishead and Clevedon ceased in the early 1930s.

Lighthouse, Portishead

67. Not only did the Ashford family farm and fish – they were also keepers of the lighthouse at Black Nore Point. Three generations of Ashfords – Joseph, James and Jim – looked after the light from the time it was built in 1894 until the last retired from the job in 1979, a total of eighty-five years. Between 1894 and 1940, the light was gas operated and had its own storage tank, fed from the village mains, which held enough for two nights so that it would not be affected by any disruption of the local supply. During those years it had to be visited twice a day in order to extinguish and light it, and also to wind up the grandfather clock-type mechanism of weights which kept the optical system revolving. In 1940 the illumination was converted to electricity, with a master switch at Nore Farm, so that it could be instantly turned off in the event of an air raid, but the clock mechanism remained until 1970 when it was changed to a system of electric motors to rotate the optics and time switches to turn the lamp on and off. Nowadays, all that is necessary is a periodic visit to keep the optical system clean.

68. By the turn of the century, it had become apparent that the days of the Bristol Training Ship 'Formidable' were numbered and steps were taken to find a site for a shore-based establishment. A lease of some fifteen acres overlooking the Channel, belonging to the Corporation of Bristol, was obtained, and plans were drawn up by Mr. Edward Gabriel, architect, for the new National Nautical School. There were great celebrations in Portishead on the occasion of the visit of H.R.H. Princess Henry of Battenberg to lay the foundation stone on 14th July 1904 – the Clevedon Mercury printed a special supplement to commemorate the event and described every aspect of the Royal visit in great detail. In less than eighteen months, this imposing building with a frontage of 382 feet and a central clock tower 90 feet high, was ready for occupation, and 350 boys moved into their new quarters on 22nd January 1906, although the formal opening ceremony did not take place until 5th May 1906, when it was performed by H.R.H. Princess Christian of Schleswig-Holstein.

National Nautical School, Portishead.

69. As shown on this photograph, the Nautical School had its own boathouse close to the beach; the gates gave access to the School's own jetty. Behind the boathouse was the outdoor swimming bath, opened in 1908, and between it and the main building were the School's playing fields on which can be seen a flagstaff and, in the distance, the mizzen mast from the Formidable, used for instructional purposes. The School's parade ground ran the length of the building, in front of it, and below it were carpenters', tailors', shoemakers' and other shops, together with the boiler room, stores, laundry, band-room and instrument store. The residence at the left-hand end was that of the captain, commanding a good view of the parade ground and playing fields. The lads slept in hammocks in four dormitories, made to resemble the deck of a vessel as far as possible. In addition to classrooms and a dining hall, the main building also housed a large gymnasium 80 feet by 50 feet, used for physical training, meetings and entertainments. Not all boys who passed through the school went to sea – some took up jobs in the other Services or entered carpentry or engineering trades, but between 1906 and 1954 more than 2,000 boys joined the Royal or Merchant Navies.

Nautical School Chapel, Portishead.

70. The Nautical School Chapel, dedicated to St. Nicholas, Patron Saint of Sailors, stands by the main entrance to the School on a site donated by the Rt. Hon. Sir William Henry Wills, Baron Winterstoke. The foundation stone was laid on 20th May 1911, and the Chapel was dedicated on 14th May 1912 in a service conducted by the Lord Bishop of Bath & Wells. Many senior Naval officers were present at the service, headed by Vice-Admiral H.S.H. Prince Louis of Battenberg, and local civic dignitaries included the Lord Lieutenant of Somerset and the Lord Mayor of Bristol. The Chapel would have been the first contact with Christian teachings experienced by many of the boys at the School, and boys were encouraged to act as servicers and choristers at the services. All Sunday services except the celebration of Holy Communion were compulsory ceremonial church parades, complete with drum and bugle band. After the closure of the establishment in 1982 as a local authority residential training school, the Chapel stood unused until 1985 when it was taken over by St. Augustine's, Redcliffe Bay, and brought back into use as St. Nicholas' C. of E. Church.

PORTISHEAD. NORE ROAD, REDCLIFF BAY. 65539

71. Until the Nautical School was built in 1904, Nore Road reached only as far as Nore Cottage – it was then extended to serve the School and Chapel. The next developments in that direction were the appearance during the 1920s of weekend residences at Redcliffe Bay – wooden huts and bungalows, typical of many other coastal developments which sprang up between the wars when local authorities had no control over building planning. This view shows Nore Road around 1930, at that time still an unmade country road, with the Nautical School Chapel in the distance. The bus is waiting for passengers at the junction with another unmade lane, now Hillside Road.

Down Channel from Redcliffe Bay, Portishead

72. This postcard shows the Redcliffe Bay area as it was during the 1920s, with Mr. Albert Heaven in the foreground. He owned land at Redcliffe Bay and was responsible for the development of the area with bungalows built mainly of timber and asbestos, situated on large plots. Although originally intended as weekend retreats, they proved very popular, many people taking up permanent residence in them even though they had neither made-up roads nor modern conveniences such as electricity and running water. Most occupants used oil for lighting and cooking until the late 1930s when electricity was installed; water had to be carried from communal taps protected by locked wooden boxes to which residents had keys. Today there are very few of these old bungalows to be seen – most were swept away during the large-scale re-development of Redcliffe Bay which took place during the 1960s and 1970s, totally changing the former character of the area, but the original developer's name lives on in Heavens Lane and Heavens Field there.

In Nightingale Valley Portishead.

73. Nightingale Valley was regarded as a local beauty spot by the Victorian and Edwardian visitors to Portishead. The steep sided ravine was flanked on the one side by the trees of Weston Big Wood and the other side by Seven Acre Wood; wild flowers grew in profusion and rare ferns were also to be found. However, in the 1920s, many trees were cleared in order to develop the Black Rock stone quarries which today bite deeply into Portishead Down. This photograph appears to have been taken when the first large trees were felled, the workers taking a break before towing away the loaded drug with the steam traction engine.

S.F.S. SERIES   RADIO STATION, PORTISHEAD   9333

74. The masts of the Radio Station on the top of Portishead Down were a prominent feature of the skyline for over fifty years until they were taken down in 1979. Operated by the Post Office, the Wireless Receiving and Transmitting Station was inaugurated in December 1927 with aerials supported by eight feet square lattice masts some 300 feet high. The Radio Station provided a long-range ship-to-shore message transmission service, and the installation had to be frequently upgraded to reflect advances in technology and to cope with the constantly increasing demands on the service – in the 1960s it was handling over half a million messages each year. In the 1970s some services were transferred to other stations at Ongar, Dorchester and Rugby, but the main service was moved to Burnham-on-Sea after closure of the Portishead station in July 1978. The name still lives on however, as the station at Burnham is known worldwide as Portishead Radio Station.

TOWER FARM
PORTISHEAD

75. Tower Farm was built by Squire Gordon, probably during the 1840s, on the fifteen acres of Portishead Down which he had acquired following the Enclosure Act of 1814. It stood in splendid isolation on the highest part of the Down, set back from Down Road, with its high stepped gables a prominent feature until it was demolished in the early 1970s to make way for the present day Tower Farm Estate. All that now remains are a few farm buildings, surrounded by modern houses. The field between Tower Farm and Down Road was known and used as the cricket field by several generations of local cricketers – one of the earliest references to it can be found in a Clevedon Mercury of 1887 when it was used for an athletics meeting to celebrate Queen Victoria's Golden Jubilee.

THE CEMETERY, PORTISHEAD.

76. Portishead acquired full Urban District status in 1895, and one of the first local problems to be considered was the urgent provision of a new burial ground. The Council's letter of 2nd November 1897 to the Home Secretary requested a warrant 'to enable the Council to borrow and expend the total sum of £1,500 to complete the purchase and lay out the Burial Ground' at the 'Chessels' site on the Weston Road. It was pointed out in the letter that because the churchyard was so full, a pathway there was having to be used for interments. The 2½ acre site was eventually developed as Portishead's cemetery, and the first burial took place in November 1899 – that of a seaman who died while his ship was in Portishead Dock. Looking towards the Down, this view was taken in the early 1900s and shows one of the gardeners working on the area just inside the stone gateway.